Franklin Watts Inc
387 Park Avenue South
New York
NY 10016

Printed in Belgium

Editor
Ruth Taylor

Picture researcher
Sarah Ridley

Designed by
Sally Boothroyd

Illustrations by
Raymond Turvey
Tony Kenyon

Photographs
Dennis Barnes pages 6-7, 13(TL), 18-19, 20-21, 21, 25;
Environmental Picture Library 23(B); Eye Ubiquitous
3, 13(TR); Friends of the Earth 24; Hutchison Library
10(T), 11(L), 12(T); Colin Molyneux 10(CR), 10(BR),
10(CL), 10(BL); Maggie Murray/Format 9, 12(B),
13(B), 19(T); Rex Features Ltd 8(L), 8(R), 23(T); Frank
Spooner Pictures Ltd 16, 17; Survival Anglia 27;
ZEFA 11(R), 14.

Acknowledgment
The author and publishers thank Tim Wood for help
with research, and Pippa Hyam, Senior Information
Officer, Friends of the Earth, for her advice.

Library of Congress Cataloging-in-Publication Data

Condon, Judith
    Recycling paper/Judith Condon
    p.cm.–(Waste control)
    Summary: Discusses the problems caused by the
manufacture and disposal of paper products, and
proposes methods for recycling them to reduce such
threats.

    ISBN 0-531-14078-4
    1. Paper industry – Environmental aspects – Juvenile literature.
    2. Waste paper – Recycling – Juvenile literature. [1. Paper
        industry – Environmental aspects. 2. Waste paper
        – Recycling.
    3. Recycling (Waste)]   I. Title.   II. Series: Waste control.
TD195.P37   1991
363.72'88 – dc20
                                    89-70742
                                       CIP
                                       AC

Recycling PAPER

Franklin Watts

New York/London/Toronto/Sydney

CONTENTS

INTRODUCTION

The problem of waste is an enormous challenge facing all modern societies. In fact, it is a problem that affects the whole of our planet.

On the one hand we are producing and consuming more and more commodities, wastefully using up the earth's natural resources such as oil and wood. On the other hand, most manufactured products, when finished with, are simply thrown away. This means that the materials and energy used to make them are lost forever. Even worse, the methods we use to dispose of this waste can create poisons which pollute soil and water, and gases which threaten our climate through "the greenhouse effect."

One way to conserve the earth's natural resources is to cut down on wasteful production. Another is to make sure that we put materials to full use, not just once, but as many times as possible. This is what recycling is all about. It means thinking about the products we use and regularly throw away; and finding ways to recover them and reuse them. This will help reduce the quantities of fresh raw materials being stripped from the earth. And every ton of material recycled is a ton kept out of the already overflowing stream of waste.

This book looks at how one important material – paper – is recycled. It describes existing programs for collecting, re-processing and reusing paper products. It explains both the advantages and the limits of recycling, and gives ideas about what more could be done.

WHAT A WASTE

This picture shows garbage being loaded onto a barge in New York. As cities run out of space, they have to dispose of garbage farther and farther away. The cost is enormous.

You may know about the problem of waste at first hand, because you have to walk every day through streets strewn with litter. Or perhaps you have seen news reports about the waste crisis in New York. This crowded city has simply run out of land on which to dump its garbage. In recent years the authorities have been loading New York's waste onto huge ships which then go off down the coast in search of a garbage dump with room to spare.

This unsightly litter was photographed in a London street, but it could be anywhere. Garbage left like this provides a breeding ground for rats

It is hard to believe that, for centuries, most of our garbage has been dumped onto open ground and then forgotten. Now the problem has caught up with us. As our towns and cities have grown, there is not enough land to spare for this kind of dumping. And even where land is available, most people understandably do not want the dump near where THEY live. Aside from being unsightly and smelly, if not properly managed these "landfill" sites can be dangerous. Rotting waste forms a chemical soup which leaks into the ground. In time, this poisonous mixture, leachate, can seep into streams and rivers. As organic waste – including paper – decomposes, it also produces a dangerous gas called methane, or "marsh gas." Some old landfills have been earthed over and then built on. It has been known for houses built on old landfill sites to start to shift as the gas builds up. At Wivenhoe, in the east of England, people had to abandon their homes which had been built on landfill. Methane had filtered up through the earth, not only causing the walls to crack, but also making the children who lived there ill.

The other main way to dispose of garbage is to burn it. This is called incineration. Large incinerators burn solid waste at very high temperatures until it is reduced to ash. Again there are problems. The garbage does not just disappear. The ash left behind still has to be dumped, and smoke from the burning process sometimes carries highly toxic chemicals such as dioxins and furans into the air. When breathed in by humans or by animals, these can cause diseases such as cancer.

By recycling paper we can greatly reduce the amount of solid waste that has to be dumped or incinerated. It has been estimated that paper (including cardboard) forms about a quarter of the weight of garbage in household garbage cans. It also forms a significant part of office and factory waste. Over a third of the total weight of solid waste in the United States is made up of paper in one form or another.

The good news is that, so long as it is kept separate from other garbage, most paper can readily be recycled. Because we use paper and paper products every day of our lives, we can all play a part. If you join in, you won't just be helping to tackle the serious problem of waste disposal. You will also be helping the environment in other ways, as the following chapters explain.

Given a choice, who would want to live near a garbage dump like this? Yet many people never bother to think where all their garbage ends up.

A birthday may make us especially aware of the amount of paper packaging we throw away. Much waste comes from over-packaging and the way goods are displayed in shops. Do small items, such as cosmetics, need elaborate wrapping? Individually wrapped portions of food and drinks are very wasteful. It is better to buy food and drink in larger units, or in concentrated form, and then serve them out at home.

ALL ABOUT PAPER

Paper and printing have formed a basis for modern civilization. These two inventions meant that knowledge could be recorded and widely spread; laws, literature, science and philosophy could be communicated across continents and oceans. Even computers rely on paper for printing out. We have also come to rely on paper packaging, from the paper bag to the cardboard box. Then there is writing paper, tissue paper, wallpaper and tracing paper – paper comes in many forms and has hundreds of uses.

Paper was first made in China 2,200 years ago. The basic process was the same as it is today. Plant fibers are suspended in water, drained through a sieve, then dried and rolled. The Chinese used mainly hemp fibers. When papermaking spread to the West, recycled textiles were used – mainly linen, then later, cotton.

A hundred years ago the demand for paper grew so fast that new milling techniques were developed, and wood fiber took over as the main raw material. In the United States at the turn of the century, 60 percent of the fibers used were from wood pulp, but 40 percent were from waste paper and rags. As the demand for paper grew, new mills were built, and new supplies of materials were sought. Fast-growing trees were specially

Pictured here is a pulp mill in Newfoundland, Canada. Huge quantities of logs are transported to the mill by boat. The wood fiber is broken down in large digestors. The pulp passes over vibrating screens until it dries and forms into paper.

planted in different parts of the world to produce wood pulp more cheaply. Often the mills were sited on riverbanks, because logs could be transported by river. The milling process also required huge quantities of water and power. The amount of recycled materials being used fell until World War II, when a huge demand for cardboard packaging meant that recycling became important again. Since then the proportion of recycled material used in papermaking has both fallen, and risen again.

The demand for wood pulp has had a big impact on the environment. In Scotland, Portugal, Brazil and Indonesia you can travel for mile upon mile and see nothing but a single species of tree, being grown for wood pulp. They are spruce or pine, or eucalyptus, depending on the climate. The trees are planted so closely together that little else survives. The balance of nature is destroyed; plants and animals lose their natural habitat; the landscape becomes monotonous and ugly.

Some people say that recycled paper saves trees. Where this means giant redwoods, poplar, beech, or birch, this is a worthwhile aim. But when it comes to the fast-growing plantations of conifers or eucalyptus, to talk of saving trees is misleading. If it were not for the demand for wood pulp these trees would not be planted in the first place. But they use up land that could be saved for natural forests, for food crops or other uses. In this case, recycling paper can help the environment by curbing the spread of single-species planting.

This hillside on Vancouver Island has been stripped of trees for papermaking. Commercial forestry on such a large scale alters the landscape and wears out the soil.

Papermaking uses vast quantities of water. Once used, this "white water" is full of chemicals and fibers, which can pollute rivers. In this settling pond the water is being treated and the scum removed.

KEEP IT SEPARATE

The first vital stage in recycling paper is to keep it separate from general waste. Once paper has become mixed with other kinds of garbage it cannot be recovered. Perhaps you already save your old newspapers and magazines for special collection, or perhaps you are involved in a voluntary paper-collecting program in your community or at school. These programs are beginning to spread. But, of course, separating and collecting paper is not the whole story. The next two stages are to repulp it, and then to make new products from it. All this involves a lot of cooperation and organization.

The word "recycle" gives a good idea of how the process works. You can think of recycling as a circle. First come the consumers – people who have used the paper and are willing to sort and separate it from the rest of their garbage. Then the paper must be collected and transported, whether by local authorities, voluntary groups or commercial dealers. Next there need to be mills ready to buy the waste, and be able to process it. Then there has to be a use for the pulped fibers – new products to be made. Finally, the circle comes back to the consumers – people wanting to buy and use those products.

Another way to describe this circle is to say that there has to be a regular "supply" of wastepaper, and there also has to be a steady "demand" for recycled paper products.

When you look more closely, you will find that there are different circles within the main circle. Paper comes in many different grades, and those grades are used for particular purposes. So, different types of

paper tend to be collected from different places. For example, the waste collected from offices and commercial premises is mainly high-quality white typing paper and computer paper. High-quality paper also comes from factories or printing works in the form of "off-cuts" – the bits left over when, for example, books are made. The waste from people's homes is mainly lower-quality paper in the form of newspapers and

magazines. The waste from stores and supermarkets is almost entirely cardboard and corrugated packaging. Each of these has to be processed in a mill designed to deal with that particular grade. And the quality of the original paper will affect the new use to which it can be put.

All this explains why the first stage – sorting and separating – is so important.

Some waste is collected from warehouses, factories and shops, as in Alfama, the old quarter of Lisbon, Portugal. Some is brought to the recycling center by members of the public, as in the picture from Wellesley, near Boston.

The wastepaper and cardboard must be sorted and graded. It is then fed onto a conveyor belt, which takes it to the bundling machines. Here it is compressed and made into bales. The bales can be stacked, and are more easily lifted by machines. They make it easier for paper to be transported in bulk to the paper mill.

Waste paper arrives at the recycling mill in enormous bales. The waste has been compressed tightly and bound with wire, so a single bale can weigh about a ton. This has the advantage that a lot of scrap can be stored in a small space, and it also helps reduce transportation costs.

A recycling mill using wastepaper or rags works in a similar way to a mill using logs or hemp (sometimes called "virgin materials"). The central idea is still to break down the raw materials so thoroughly that all the tiny fibers are separated and weakened. Just as when wood chips are used, the waste is mixed with huge quantities of water and reduced to a pulp, before being passed through tanks to be cleaned. It is easy to see that breaking down wastepaper is quicker and easier than breaking down wood. This is one way that savings of fuel and energy are made.

However, pulp made from recycled paper does present an important problem of its own. People who give their wastepaper for recycling are asked to remove things such as paper clips or rubber bands, and mills recycling magazines have a way to remove staples. Other things are harder to get rid of. Mixed in with the fibers are various substances added when the original product was made. Nonsolvent glues are particularly difficult to deal with as they clog up the pulping equipment. This is why bulky telephone directories and catalogs, which are bound with lots of glue, are unsuitable for repulping. Perhaps the most obvious contaminant of wastepaper is printer's ink. In order to remove it, detergents are bubbled through the pulp in a process called "de-inking." The pulp may also be bleached, or whitened, with chlorine, hydrogen peroxide or sulfur dioxide. It then has to be washed and mixed again, before going forward to be sieved and dried.

pulp mixture enters the machine here

much of the water drains away as mixture is gently shaken over a wire mesh

suction rollers draw off more water

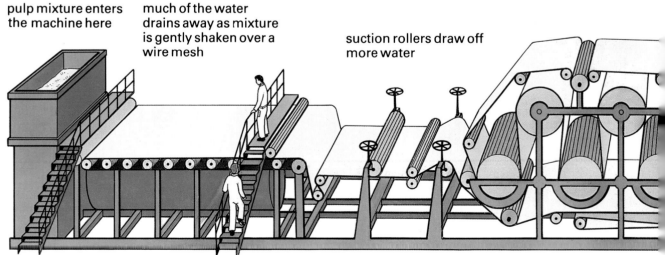

Left behind is a sludge full of chemicals, detergent, bleaching agents, and ink. If discharged into rivers and lakes, this sludge can poison plant and animal life. It, too, needs to be treated and disposed of responsibly. Unfortunately, some paper mills have a bad record of causing the pollution of inland waterways. The process of recycling is not without hazards.

As we have seen, the various grades of wastepaper are recycled separately and put to specific uses. It is not possible to make fine art paper out of old newspapers, for instance. Low-quality fiber is suitable for making newsprint, or fiberboard, or egg cartons. High-quality fiber can be recycled into stationery – writing paper, envelopes, office paper. Other grades go into the making of packaging, paper tissues, toilet rolls and kitchen paper. Some products, including egg cartons, insulation materials, low-quality newsprint and packaging, are made entirely of recycled materials. But it is more usual for pulp from recycled fibers to be mixed with pulp from "virgin" materials. The reason for this is explained in the following section.

This picture shows part of a paper pulp de-inking factory. Water used in the de-inking process is being treated, and the scum scooped off.

Modern papermaking machines can be up to 656 feet long
▽

Recycled paper, or partly recycled paper, is used to make a wide variety of products, including those used in the office. Many manufacturers are keen to add labels stating that their products have been made from recycled materials, or are able to be recycled.

felt-covered rollers press the paper

hot cylinders dry the paper

the finished paper is wound onto large reels

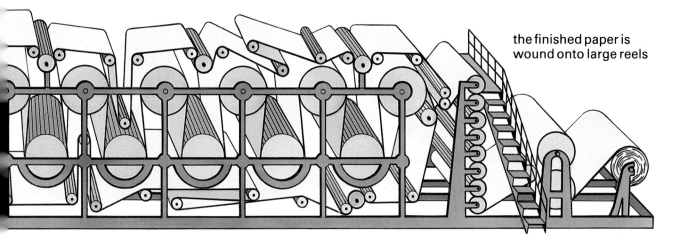

WHAT'S THE LIMIT?

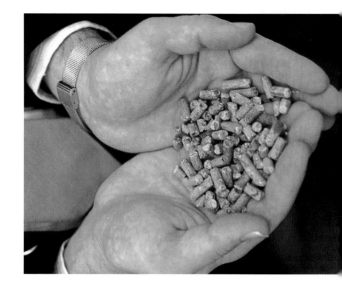

You may by now be wondering what happens when paper made from recycled paper is finished with? Can it be recycled again? In other words, can paper be recycled indefinitely?

The simple answer to this last question is no. Although some types of paper can be recycled several times over, there is a limit. Plant fibers, including wood and cotton, are made up of cellulose. Each time they are pulped, the fibers become shorter and weaker. Once they have reached the very lowest grade, any further pulping would be useless. Anything made from them would tend to crumble and fall apart.

Fibers in the lowest grade are suitable for products that will not be recycled. One obvious example is toilet paper, which is disposed of through the sewage system. But

there is another way to tackle the problem of deterioration in the case of white paper. This is to make sure that paper which is likely to be recycled always contains a proportion of "virgin" material. For example, some paper is made from half new fibers and half once-recycled material. When this paper is itself recycled, it can be mixed with virgin fiber again, half and half. This time the paper produced will be made up of one quarter of once-recycled fibers, and one quarter of twice-recycled fibers; but one half will still be new fibers. And so on.

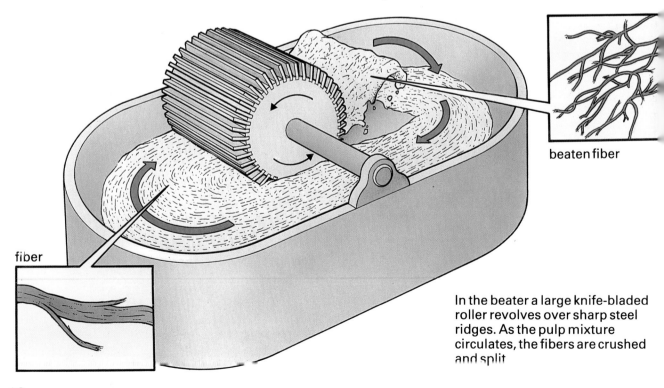

fiber

beaten fiber

In the beater a large knife-bladed roller revolves over sharp steel ridges. As the pulp mixture circulates, the fibers are crushed and split

A new process invented in France compacts general waste into small, dry pellets. These are easy to handle and can be stored without rotting.

The pellets can be used to make building blocks and other construction materials.

Another limit is caused by wastage. Even when paper is put into a recycling mill, not all of it finds its way through to the end of the process. A lot of the fibers are washed out along the way, as the paper is pulped, and de-inked. Altogether, it takes about one and a third tons of paper waste to make one ton of recycled paper.

Some paper cannot be recycled because of the use to which it is put. Toilet paper has already been mentioned. Paper tissues, disposable diapers, wallpaper, and paper contaminated with food waste are other examples of paper products that cannot be recycled.

Another constraint is caused by the way some paper is processed. Plastic film or metal lining is added to paper cartons for fruit juice; other products are made of paper coated with wet-strength resins, or adhesives, or wax. Unfortunately, these and other contaminants make pulping more difficult, and cause damage to papermaking equipment. They are widely used, and often without good reason. The result is that most of the paper treated with them can never be recycled.

None of the paper products used at this picnic can be recycled. This is because of the way they have been made, or because of the use to which they have been put.

WHAT DOES IT COST?

In some cases wastepaper is cheaper to buy than wood. The pulping of waste uses less energy, and this means financial savings. Making paper from recycled rather than virgin fibers also involves the use of less water and fewer chemicals. Cleaning contaminated water costs money too. So, recycling brings direct benefits to the paper industry.

However, to see the full benefits of recycling, we need to look much wider. To take just one example, it has been calculated that pulping waste rather than wood brings energy savings of between a quarter and a half. This is good for us all, because most of the energy used in paper mills comes from the burning of fossil fuels – which adds to the greenhouse effect and to acid rain; or else from nuclear power stations – which create radioactive waste. How is it possible to put a simple money value on things that affect the health of the whole planet?

At the same time, it is important to realize that environmental savings are relative. That is to say, collecting and recycling paper is not done without cost, even if the cost is hidden. For example, if every family drives its waste paper by car two or three miles to a collection point each week, that is costly in terms of time, gas, and exhaust pollution. So recycling has to be organized in a sensible way.

Emissions from power stations, factories and vehicle exhausts add to the greenhouse effect, leading to hotter and drier seasons in many parts of the world. Here a crop of soybeans in Ohio has failed because of drought conditions during 1988. Who can calculate the real cost of such global changes?

When individual companies make decisions, they are more likely to do what is best for profits than to think about global issues. Their aim is to keep costs down and to be more efficient. Where there is a good and regular supply of wastepaper, someone may decide to use it to make new paper or paperboard. But developing technology to process even more waste, or switching production to recycled products, both need investment. Some companies are cynical about their wider responsibilities to the environment. In Sweden, for example, one mill was found to be discharging illegal levels of pollution. Unwilling to spend money on improvements, the company instead moved to Brazil, where the law is less strict.

In the same way, individual countries put their own economic needs first. What makes good economic sense to a high waste-producer may be bad for a country that grows trees for pulp. In the United States, Japan, and parts of Europe, collecting and selling waste paper is a profitable industry. The United States exports over 6,000,000 tons of wastepaper a year to places such as Korea and Taiwan, and this could more than double by 1995. On the other hand, poor countries produce very little surplus waste. Here people value every scrap of material they can get hold of, sometimes even making their homes from cardboard packing cases.

Rapid industrial development in some countries has brought people from rural areas to the cities. Here they are forced to live as best they can, often from what others throw away. This shanty town in Kenya is one of many where the houses are made from old packing cases.

From the UK *Daily Telegraph*, January 5 1990.

At present in the United States waste computer paper is worth around $200-$300 a ton, and printing and photocopying paper around $700. When stocks of waste build up, the price paid for it falls, affecting voluntary collectors and paper-merchants alike. If it is not financially worthwhile, they stop collecting and a shortage develops. Then the price goes up again. Many people believe that recycling is far too important to be left to these commercial ups and downs.

£300m straw mill scheme would create jobs for 850

By Roger Highfield
Science Editor

A PLAN to set up a £300 million straw pulp mill next to the Humber estuary was announced yesterday.

If it receives Government backing, the project will create 850 jobs and reduce the amount of straw currently burned in Britain by a third.

Eurosell, a subsidiary of Berisford Bristar, is to put a planning application for the plant near Grimsby before Cleethorpes Borough Council and Humberside County Council.

However, even if the application receives approval, the project will not necessarily go ahead. The final decision will be made in six months and will depend on Government financial support, said Mr Bob Bass, Eurocell director.

If the proposal receives approval and backing the plant could be built by the end of 1992. It would create 250 permanent jobs and 600 more within the local community.

The plant would convert 750,000 tonnes of straw into 300,000 tonnes of high quality paper pulp each year. The process involved is similar to pulping wood. The fibre contains lignin, cellulose and hemi-cellulose. Cellulose will be extracted for paper production and the waste lignin liquor burned to provide almost all the energy the mill needs.

The company claims that it would greatly reduce the 2·5 million tonnes of straw burned each year, a major agricultural nuisance, and would help reduce imports of hard wood pulp.

We have looked at paper being wastefully dumped, and paper being recycled into paper. But there are some other, indirect, ways in which paper is recycled.

In parts of Europe and in America there are now several large incinerators able to burn waste – including plastics and paper – and extract energy in the form of heat. There are currently more than 120 of these waste-to-energy plants in operation in the United States, and 30 more being built. In Britain, at the Coventry Waste Reduction Unit, the heat produced from burning municipal waste is converted into steam and then passed through a heat exchanger to heat water for the Peugeot Talbot factory a third of a mile away. Another enormous incinerator at Edmonton, north London, uses heat from the burning of waste to generate electricity. Incinerators in Nottingham and Sheffield produce energy for British Coal, and for district heating.

There are serious problems with incineration. The incinerators cost a great deal to construct, and they produce toxic fumes and ash. The maintaining of very high temperatures, and the use of cleaning and scrubbing equipment, can help reduce the fumes that escape. But these controls make the process much more costly. When it comes to supplying direct heat power, the customer has to be near the incinerator, or else too much energy is lost in transfer. Nevertheless, with technological improvements, waste-to-heat generation will become increasingly important. Paper which cannot be separated from the general waste stream will help in the production of energy. Since much waste does have to be

burned, it is obviously worthwhile to try to find ways of recycling the energy released.

Another useful development has been the extracting of methane from landfills. As we have seen, organic waste, including paper, produces this gas as it rots. Some landfill sites now have the capacity to extract the gas and use it to generate electricity. One such landfill in Michigan extracts enough methane to produce 33,000 kilowatts of electricity a day – enough to power 1,800 homes as well as its own buildings. These include a one-acre plastic greenhouse, powered entirely by the methane, and weighing so little that it does not press down on the landfill beneath. Here salad greens and herbs are grown.

Under the right conditions, shredded waste-paper can also be mixed with vegetable and garden waste to be composted, and used as a growing medium for plants. It can even be processed to extract its protein for animal feedstuffs, and to make ethyl alcohol and various chemicals. Meanwhile, some old landfill sites, once made safe, are being turned into ski slopes and leisure centers.

Mount Trashmore near Detroit is a landfill site from which methane is extracted to generate electricity for 2,000 homes. The 160-foot high landfill has been earthed over for use as a ski-slope.

Once imagination is applied to the problem of finding uses for wastepaper, the list seems to grow and grow. You may yourself have made papier-mâché containers or craft items, pasting small scraps of paper onto a mold to create the shape. All kinds of masks, stage props and cheap jewelry can be made in this way.

Shredded paper can be baled like straw and used like straw for animal bedding. Together with manure, it can also be spread on the land as a mulch and fertilizer.

◁ Gardeners recycle kitchen waste by stacking it in layers with soil or ash, open to the air. Heat builds up inside, and the waste decomposes into a dark brown crumbly mixture called compost. This is used to feed growing flowers and vegetables.

RECYCLING IN ACTION

As we have seen, recycling paper is not a new idea. For decades the paper industry in different parts of the world has been geared, at least in part, to using wastepaper as a resource.

Japan has a massive, sophisticated network of paper recycling and claims a 50 percent recovery rate. Households are asked to sort and separate garbage before collection. In Tokyo dealers tour neighborhoods collecting newspapers and magazines and offering toilet and facial tissues in return. In Holland, 57 percent of the fiber used in papermaking comes from waste. West Germany, too, has a strong record, encouraged by its influential "green" consumer movement.

Sixty percent of the paper and board bought and used in Britain is imported. The paper at present made in British mills is mainly lower-grade, and for this just over half the

raw material is waste paper. The British paper industry is aiming to double its output in coming years. A huge plant using 25 percent recycled fiber has been brought into production in Shotton, on the Wirral, and the demand for recycled paper is growing. The United States now claims to be recycling 30 percent of all paper consumed. Early in 1990 the American paper industry set itself the goal of increasing this to 40 percent within six years.

Some countries believe that they already collect and recycle as much high-grade paper as they possibly can, most of it in bulk from paper manufacturers, printers, businesses and government offices. The biggest single category of wastepaper collected is made up of cardboard and corrugated boxes of the kind used to transport goods to stores, supermarkets and factories. In some American cities as much as 60 percent of all such packaging is recovered for recycling. Many stores and supermarkets even have their own simple balers into which boxes are fed, ready for collection.

In some places items able to be recycled are set out on the curbside, ready for collection. Paper, glass, aluminum and recyclable plastics need to be kept separate.

Obviously there are still improvements to be made in the recycling of both these important grades. But the biggest opportunity for increased recycling comes from household waste, especially newspapers and magazines. Here, municipal programs and those run by local organizations or charities have come into their own. Recent technological advances have helped, by making the reprocessing of newsprint and magazine paper easier. The increasing use of water-soluble ink makes de-inking much less hazardous and less costly. And many reprocessing plants now have the ability to remove staples mechanically.

In addition to these developments, there is a growing awareness on the part of consumers that they should buy products made with recycled paper, and by the same token avoid products that are nonrecyclable. Anxious to be part of this popular mood, and to adopt a "green image," more and more companies are making a virtue of the fact that they use recycled paper, whereas before they might have kept the fact hidden. The large supermarket chain "Safeway," for example, has proudly claimed that the 11,000,000 brown "Treesaver" bags it provides each year for its customers are made of recycled paper. Other companies are labeling goods as either made from recycled paper, or able to be recycled.

Retailing companies promote a "green" image by providing bags made of recycled paper.

A local paper collection run by Friends of the Earth in Bristol, England.

HOW GOVERNMENTS CAN HELP

Since recycling paper can bring so many benefits to society as a whole, local and national governments should take measures to encourage it.

Many city programs have been established with official backing. One example is in Britain, where the environmental group Friends of the Earth has pioneered a recycling program in the cities of Sheffield and Cardiff. The plan is for local authorities, central government, and voluntary organizations to work together. Government departments have given financial support, and so has the British Telecom company. Households are given a blue box in which to put out cans, bottles, and plastic containers for collection. They are asked to put out newspapers and magazines separately, tied in bundles, next to the blue box. It is hoped that other cities will follow suit.

In one American city, Seattle, the authorities charge households $13.75 to have a single garbage can emptied once a month, and $9 for each extra can. Private haulers collect recyclable materials and garden waste, which are left out separately. Having to pay according to how much waste they throw out means that most people have switched to buying goods with less packaging; and when possible they choose recyclables. Two thirds of residents signed up to join the recycling program. In fact, people were so eager to join that, to begin with, there was a long waiting list! In Woodbury, New Jersey, people not separating recyclables from their general waste receive a warning from the authorities

If they break the law again, their garbage is simply not collected. If they continue, they can be fined up to $300.

At national or state level, laws have been passed both to try to "manage the waste stream," and to encourage recycling. Managing the waste stream means trying to make things so that they will be easy to recycle. One way to encourage this is to pass laws about the materials to be used, and about not mixing materials. Only governments or international bodies have a big enough overview to create a total waste strategy. The Council of the European Community has adopted a resolution on waste prevention, recycling, and disposal, but implementation is still a long way off.

When it comes to paper, government departments and agencies are themselves huge – and often wasteful – consumers. One obvious way to set a good example is to see that all government offices, and even schools buy recycled paper. This is called a procurement policy. Over 30 states in America have taken this step.

Blue boxes of recyclable waste left out for collection by householders in Sheffield, England.

Meanwhile, other states have introduced special taxes on products that cause litter, and have banned certain materials from landfills. In Oregon, tax allowances exist for companies making an effort to use recycled materials, and they are also helped with low-interest loans and grants. The authorities also set goals. This means that all companies are in the same boat; some cannot save money by doing nothing to help. For example, the state of Florida has introduced a tax to be paid on newsprint if the level of recycling does not reach 50 percent by 1993, and California and Connecticut have similar rising targets. All these measures help to increase public awareness and people's commitment to recycling.

◁ This greenhouse is being powered entirely by electricity generated by methane gas. The methane is drawn from decayed garbage in an old landfill site.

A better way to collect garbage: this municipal garbage truck pulls a trailer with separate compartments for recyclables.

PART OF THE SOLUTION

There are many problems in the world which we feel powerless to do anything about. But when it comes to the problem of waste, there ARE things we can all do to help. Each one of us can avoid buying and using wasteful products, or products wastefully packaged. We can all do our best to recycle paper in a variety of ways. And when we have a choice, we can buy paper products made from recycled fiber.

Here is a list of suggestions of how you can help. You will probably be able to add other ideas of your own.

a) BUYING Choose to buy eggs in cardboard boxes, drink in glass bottles, and recycled paper products.

When buying:

Avoid all overpackaged items, whether food, stationery, toiletries or cosmetics. Fast-food is a particularly bad offender, and probably not very good for you either!

Talk to the person in your house who shops for household items such as toilet tissue. Ask him or her to check if these are made of recycled paper.

Whenever possible, buy drinks in returnable bottles. Avoid paper cartons covered in wax or plastic, which cannot be recycled. Buy concentrated drinks and dilute them at home.

Buy eggs in cardboard rather than plastic cartons.

Whenever possible, buy recycled writing paper, note paper and drawing paper.

Check what your school does to reduce waste. Does it buy recycled paper?

b) REUSING You can often find ways of reusing paper and books.

This is an ancient mixed forest in Poland, photographed as the colors begin to change in autumn. Trees of several varieties combine to provide food and shelter for animals, large and small. Compare its beauty with the photograph of a logged hillside on page 11. Could you become part of the solution – helping to save our precious natural environment?

When using:

Write on both sides of the paper whenever possible. Use a pencil and eraser, especially when drafting work. Use up the backs of old handouts and letters.

Save scraps of clean paper. Staple them together to make your own telephone- or memo-pad.

Reuse envelopes. Gummed paper is not suitable for recycling.

Make full use of your local library – the best way ever invented to recycle books!

Share books and magazines with your friends. Set up a swap-shop at school. Give books you have finished with to younger children or thrift shops or the local hospital.

Try to become more aware of all the paper that comes into your house and think if it is really needed. For example, do you send off for too many mail-order catalogs, most of which are heavily glued and not recyclable? Ask those you live with if they ever read the junk mail delivered each week. If not, suggest writing to the senders requesting that your family's name be removed from their mailing lists.

Collecting

Find out what recycling programs already exist in your community. If there is a curb-side collection program, remember to tie your paper in bundles or place it in bags, and leave it out on the right day.

If there is no collection program, perhaps there is a recycling center or collection point you can take wastepaper to.

Suggest to your scout troop or school that they start collecting wastepaper to raise funds. First you will need to check that there is a nearby paper-merchant willing to buy it from you. You will also need a safe place, under cover, to store the paper where it will not be a fire hazard.

If no programs exist, or if they are inadequate, write to your local government officials or your Congressional representative, to suggest the benefits of recycling.

Finally, remember, recycling needs you to make it work!

GLOSSARY

acid rain   polluted rain which kills trees and poisons lakes; caused by smoke from the burning of fossil fuels, especially by power stations

bale   square-sided bundle made by compressing material in a frame

bleaching agent   chemical substance which acts on materials making them appear whiter

cancer   disease of animals and humans in which cells of the body multiply out of control

cellulose   basic substance of which plant cells are made

compost   crumbly, nutrient-rich mixture on which plants can be grown

detergent   cleansing agent with ability to make oil-based substances combine with water

dioxin   by-product of incineration; one of the most poisonous substances on earth: kills plant and animal life, even in minute quantities

effluent   liquid waste flowing from mills or factories

ethyl alcohol   a colorless liquid, 100 percent alcohol, used in the making of dyes, pharmaceuticals and antifreeze

European Community   organization of European countries committed to free trade

fossil fuels   substances such as coal and oil, formed from ancient forests and vegetation; a nonrenewable energy source

furan   poisonous chemical by-product of incineration

green   name of certain European political parties and popular movements concerned with protecting the environment

greenhouse effect   potentially disastrous warming of the earth's climate, brought about by gases holding more of the sun's heat in the atmosphere

hemp   fibrous plant from which rope and paper can be made

incineration   process of burning in a furnace at high temperatures to reduce materials by both weight and volume

landfill   place where garbage is dumped on open ground, often in valley or hollow

leachate   poisonous mixture of chemicals which seeps from base of garbage dumps

methane   "marsh gas"; explosive and smelly gas made when organic waste rots

newsprint   paper on which newspapers are printed

organic waste   waste consisting of materials that once grew naturally in plant or animal form

papier mâché   the modeling of objects from torn scraps of paper, which are wetted, then pasted onto a mold before trimming and painting

procurement policy   decision to buy goods of a certain type or from a certain source

single-species planting   forestry consisting of one type of tree suitable for industrial use

virgin material/fiber   raw material not previously processed or used in manufacture

voluntary program   a program in which people participate out of good will or for a good cause

ADDRESSES AND RESOURCES

American Paper Institute, Inc., 206 Madison Avenue, New York, NY 10016

Conservatree Paper Company, 10 Lombard Street, Suite 250, San Francisco, CA 94111

Environmental Defense Fund, 1616 P Street, NW, Washington, DC 20036

Greenpeace, USA, 1611 Connecticut Avenue, NW, Washington, DC 20009

Pollution Probe, 12 Madison Avenue, Toronto, Ontario M5R 2SI, Canada

U.S. Environmental Protection Agency, 401 M Street, SW, Washington, DC 20460

World Watch Institute, 1776 Massachusetts Avenue, NW, Washington, DC 20036

INDEX

PRINTED IN BELGIUM BY
proost
INTERNATIONAL BOOK PRODUCTION